Potatoes

101 Quick Easy and Delicious Recipes

Copyright © Rajni Khurana 2007

Published 2007 by
Rupa & Co
7/16 Ansari Road, Daryaganj
New Delhi 110 002

Sales Centres:
Allahabad Bangalore Chandigarh Chennai
Hyderabad Jaipur Kathmandu Kolkata Mumbai Pune

All rights reserved
No part of this publication may be reproduced, stored
in a retrieval system, or transmitted in any form or by
any means, electronic, mechanical, photocopying,
recording or otherwise without the prior permission of
the publishers.

Book design by Sonali Lal
(sonalilal@gmail.com)

Photographs by Prabhat Gupta, Pawan Narang

Food Styling by Rajni Khurana, Prabhat Gupta

Illustration by Vishala Khurana

Printed in India by
Nutech Photolithographers, New Delhi

Potatoes

101 Quick Easy and Delicious Recipes

Rajni Khurana

Rupa & Co

Contents

History of the Potato	7
Introduction	8

Potatoes in Appetizers
- Tandoori Aloo Tikka — 10
- Cheesy stuffed potato — 11
- Potato Chip cookies — 12
- Patrani Aloo — 13
- Thai Potatoes — 14
- Potato Sate — 15
- Sesame Potatoes on Toast — 16
- Potato Spinach Rolls — 17
- Vegetable Seekh Kababs — 18
- Potato Salt-Pepper — 18
- Cajun Oven Fried Potatoes — 19
- Schezwan Potato Rolls — 20
- Potato Papad Rolls — 20
- Pot Roast Potatoes — 21

Potatoes in Soups
- Mexican Chilli Potato Soup — 22
- Cheesy Potato Soup — 23
- Potato and Corn Chowder — 24
- Potato and Leek Soup — 25
- Jamaican Pepper Pot Soup — 26
- Green Spring Soup — 27
- Country Style Potato And Lentil Soup — 28
- Potato Pesto Soup — 29
- Spinach and Potato Soup — 30
- Curried Potato Soup — 31

Potatoes in Salads
- Bean And Potato Salad — 32
- Hot Potato Salad — 33
- German Potato Salad — 34
- Black and White Salad — 35
- Hawaiian Potato Salad — 36
- Swedish Potato Salad — 37
- Potato and Sweet Potato Salad with Ginger Orange Dressing — 38
- Creamy Minted Potato — 39
- Mediterranean Potato Platter — 40
- Potato Waldorf Salad — 41

Potatoes in Rice and Roti Dishes
- Kashmiri Aloo Pulao — 42
- Aloo Masala Bhaat — 43
- Aloo Biryani — 44
- Potato and Tomato Rice — 45
- Green Aloo Pulao — 46
- Minty Potato Pulao — 46
- Potato Puris — 47
- Potato Cheese Parathas — 48
- Aloo Gobhi Parathas — 49

Potatoes in Indian Main Course
- Aloo Papad Mangodi — 50
- Potato Dum Pukht — 51
- Moghlai Aloo — 52
- Hyderabadi Aloo — 53
- Kerela Potato Stew — 54

- Aloo Posto — 54
- Aloo Kurma — 55
- Aloo Kofta in Mattar Gravy — 56
- Aloo Mattar Kheema — 57
- Aloo Do Pyaaza — 58
- Khatte Aloo — 59
- Goan Potato Curry — 60
- Red Hot Potatoes — 61
- Quick and Easy Potato Curry — 62
- Shahi Aloo Bharta — 63
- Tilwale Aloo — 64
- Sponge Curry — 65

Potatoes in International Main Course

- Potato Gnocchi — 66
- Potato Florentine — 67
- Patatas Bravas- Spanish Potatoes — 68
- Creole Potatoes — 68
- Potato and Onion Casserole — 69
- Kung Pao Potatoes — 70
- Roast Potatoes — 71
- Potato and Cauliflower Goulash — 72
- Potato and Mushroom Au Gratin — 73
- Chilly Garlic Potatoes — 74
- Potato Cheese Pie — 75
- Deluxe Potato Bake — 76
- Potato Manchurian — 77
- Potato Siciliana — 78
- Pesto Potato Bake — 79

Potatoes in One Dish Meals

- Potato Pizza — 80
- Potato Mushroom Enchiladas — 81
- Baked Potato — 82
- Potato Gado Gado Salad — 83
- Spanish Omelette — 84
- Aloo Frankee Rolls — 84
- Potato Pancake Rolls — 85
- Potato Pancake — 86
- Eggs Flamenco — 86
- Potato Kathee Rolls — 87

Potatoes in Chaats

- Diet Aloo Chaat — 88
- Bread Aloo Bhel — 89
- Aloo Paapdi Chaat — 90
- Biscuit Chaat — 91
- Berhampuri Paapdi Chaat — 92
- Benarasi Aloo Chaat — 93
- Sprout Bhel — 94
- Aloo Vada Chaat — 95
- Aloo Corn Bhel — 96
- Aloo Palak Chaat — 97
- Ragda Patties — 98
- Chutneys — 99

Potatoes in Fasting

- Aloo Khichdi — 100
- Sabudana Vada — 101
- Sabudana Khichdi — 102
- Stuffed Aloo Tikki — 102
- Sabudana Paratha — 103

History of the Potato

Cultivated potatoes all belong to one botanical species, "solanum tubersum" But it includes thousands of varieties that vary by size, shape, colour and other sensory characteristics.

The potato originated in the South American Andes about 4500 years ago. 16 century Spanish explorers first observed the potato in Peru, Bolivia, Colombia and Eucador. The first specimens probably reached Spain around 1570. From there the potato spread via herbalists and farmers to Italy, the low countries and England. There was a second introduction sometime in the following 20 years.

An Irish forklore credits Sir Francis Drake with introducing the potato to Great Britain. On his round the world voyage (1577-1580) he recorded an encounter with potatoes of the Chilean coast in 1578.

By 1650 potatoes were a field crop in Flanders and they had spread northward to Zeeland, Urecht, Overijssel and Friesland. The harsh winter of 1740 which caused damage to other crops hastened potato planting everywhere.

By 1794 the tubers were an element of the Dutch national dish, a hot pot of root vegetables. Towards the end of the 18 century, potatoes had become a field crop in Germany. There popularity was increased by natural disasters and also by the disasters of wars, because the tubers could be kept in the ground where stores were less likely subject to looting and burning by marauding armies.

From mid 18-19 centuries potatoes finally spread across Central and Eastern Europe into Russia and the rest of the world.

Introduction

Potato is a vegetable that needs no introduction. One of the most versatile vegetables available in the market, potatoes are easy to prepare and store very well, which makes them an extremely convenient ingredient to have at all times. Very popular with children, no meal seems complete without a potato dish.

It is only a myth that potatoes are fattening. Potatoes are virtually fat free, unless of course deep fried. Besides, potatoes combine energy giving complex carbohydrates with plenty of Vitamin C, fiber and potassium. In fact, a baked potato supplies more than twice as much potassium as a banana.

How to buy:
At the market, look for potatoes that are smooth, well shaped and firm. They

should be free from blemishes and sprouts. Avoid those with green skin, cracks and discoloration.

How to prepare:
Scrub potatoes well under cold, running water. To boil, heat some water in a pan and put the potatoes in. Cover and allow to cook. This preserves the vitamin C in the potatoes. Small potatoes take 10-15 minutes to cook, large ones take about 20-30 minutes. Alternately boil potatoes in a pressure cooker. In the cooker, small potatoes would take 5-7 minutes under pressure, whereas large ones would take 12-15 minutes.

Cooking potatoes in a microwave is a healthy way to cook them. For microwaving, pierce 4 whole potatoes in several places. Microwave on high for 13-15 minutes.

How to eat:
It's a good idea to eat potatoes with the skin, as some of the nutrients are concentrated in or just under the skin. Alternately, peel them after cooking. Potatoes can be eaten boiled, baked or fried or in the 101 ways that I have suggested. Keep turning the pages and discover different ways of preparing delicious potato dishes. All in my quick and easy style of course.

All the recipes are for serving 4-6 people depending on the number of dishes being presented at your table. The oil to use would be any vegetable cooking oil. Though I would recommend olive oil particularly for salads and stir fry dishes.

Do enjoy creating these dishes as much as I enjoyed putting them together.

APPETIZERS

Tandoori Aloo Tikka

Ingredients:

4-6 potatoes, boiled and peeled
½ cup thick dahi
1 teaspoon ginger garlic paste
1 teaspoon chilli powder
½ teaspoon haldi powder
½ teaspoon jeera powder
½ teaspoon garam masala powder
½ teaspoon chaat masala
½ teaspoon black salt
Pinch of red tandoori color (optional)
Salt to taste
Onion slices and lemon wedges to garnish.

Method:

- Mix all the dry masalas into the dahi.
- Cut the potatoes into large cubes and mix in the marinade.
- Keep in the fridge for 2-3 hours.
- At the time of serving, place the marinated potato cubes on a foil lined oven tray and grill on high heat for 5-6 minutes.
- Serve hot garnished with onion rings and lemon.

Cheesy Stuffed Potato

Ingredients:

4-6 potatoes, boiled
4 tablespoons grated cheese
½ cup milk
¼ teaspoon mustard powder

4 tablespoons baked beans (optional)
Salt and pepper to taste
Chilly powder to garnish

Method:
- Cut the potatoes into half without peeling them.
- Scoop out the centre portion of the potatoes leaving a shell all around.
- Mash the scooped out portion of the potatoes, along with cheese, milk, mustard powder, baked beans if using and seasoning.
- Fill this mixture into the scooped out shells and sprinkle the chilly powder on top.
- Bake or grill till golden brown and serve hot.

Potato Chip Cookies

Ingredients:
50 gms potato chips
100 gm grated cheese
2 teaspoons til
100 gms flour
¾ teaspoon mustard powder
Pinch chilli powder
60 gms melted butter

Method:
- Preheat the oven to 180°C.
- Put the potato chips in a bowl along with the cheese, and mix well, crushing the chips.
- Add the sesame seeds, sifted flour, mustard and chilli powder.
- Mix in the butter and form a dough.
- Make small balls and place on a greased tray.
- Bake for about 15 minutes.
- Serve preferably the same day.

Patrani Aloo

Ingredients:
4-5 boiled potatoes
3-4 tablespoons green chutney
1-2 tablespoons dahi
salt to taste

Method:
- Peel and cut the potatoes into cubes and mix in the dahi, chutney and salt.
- Wrap the mixture in a banana leaf.
- Tie with string and steam.
- Alternately put the potatoes into a piece of foil, make into a parcel and steam

I have adapted this recipe from the Parsi- Patrani Machhi. Low in calories, it's the perfect diet snack.

Thai Potatoes

Ingredients:

1 packet baby potatoes boiled
1 tablespoon butter
1 small bundle lemon grass
4-5 spring onions finely chopped
Salt to taste
1 cup coconut milk

For the green paste:
8-10 cloves garlic
2 teaspoons pepper corns
1 cup fresh coriander
2 tablespoon lemon juice
$\frac{1}{4}$ cup peanuts

Method:
- Grind the ingredients for the paste.
- Put the butter in a pan and add the potatoes, lemon grass, spring onion and salt and cook.
- When done, add the green paste and coconut milk and cook till dry.
- Serve hot on toothpicks.

Try making this into a curry. Add 2 more cups of coconut milk along with a cup of water and boil.

Potato Sate

Ingredients:

1 packet baby potatoes
Boiled and peeled
3 capsicums
3 onions
3 tomatoes

Marinade:
4 tablespoons soya sauce
4 tablespoons lime juice
2 cloves garlic (crushed)
1 teaspoon chilly powder
1 tablespoon sugar

Peanut sauce:
1 cup peanuts
4 cloves garlic (chopped)
1 cup coconut milk
2 tablespoons soya sauce
2 tablespoons brown sugar
$\frac{1}{4}$ cup Lemon juice
1 teaspoon chilly powder
1 teaspoon oil

Method:

- Mix all the ingredients for the marinade.
- Marinate the vegetables and thread onto skewers alternating the potatoes, onion, tomato and capsicum.
- To prepare the sauce, grind the peanuts coarsely in a mixer.
- Heat the oil and stir fry the garlic.
- Add the rest of the ingredients and cook for a few minutes, adding a little water or coconut milk if needed.
- Serve with the potato skewers.

Sesame Potato on Toast

Ingredients:
4 slices bread
2 potatoes, boiled and mashed
2 spring onions finely chopped
1 tablespoon chopped garlic
1 tablespoon chopped ginger
1 green chilly finely chopped

1 teaspoon soy sauce
2 tablespoons sesame seeds
3 tablespoons flour
Salt to taste
Pinch of ajinomoto (optional)
Oil for deep frying

Method:
- Mix together the potatoes, spring onions, garlic, ginger, green chilly and soy sauce.
- Season with salt and ajinomoto if using.
- Spread this mixture over the 4 bread slices.
- Mix the flour with 4-5 tablespoons of water to make a paste.
- Spread the flour paste over the potatoes covering them well.
- Sprinkle over the sesame seeds.
- Fry in hot oil and serve.

Potato Spinach Rolls

Ingredients:
4 potatoes, boiled
1 onion, chopped
2 green chillies, chopped
Coriander leaves, chopped
Few drops lemon juice
20-25 spinach leaves
1 cup besan
Salt and chilly powder to taste
Oil for deep frying

Method:
- Mash the potatoes and mix in the onion, green chilly, coriander leaves, lemon juice and salt to taste.
- Shape into rolls.
- Place a small roll of the potato filling in the centre of each spinach leaf and roll up each leaf.
- Make a batter of the besan using water.
- Season with salt and chilly powder.
- Heat the oil for deep frying.
- Dip each roll into the batter and fry.
- Serve hot.

Keep the rolls ready in advance and fry hot just before serving.

Vegetable Seekh Kababs

Ingredients:

3 potatoes, boiled
2 cups mixed vegetables, boiled
2 teaspoons ginger garlic paste
1 onion, finely chopped
2 green chillies, finely chopped
2 tablespoons coriander leaves
2 slices bread, crumbled
Salt and garam masala to taste
Oil to baste
Chaat masala and onion rings to garnish

Method:
- Mash the potatoes along with the boiled vegetables.
- Add in the ginger garlic paste, onion, green chilly, coriander, bread and seasoning.
- Mix well to make a stiff dough.
- If the dough is too soft, add some more bread.
- Roll portions of the mixture onto bamboo skewers.
- Pour some oil over the kababs and grill until golden.
- Sprinkle chaat masala and serve hot.

Potatoes Salt-Pepper

Ingredients:

2 large potatoes
2 tablespoons cornflour
Salt and pepper
Pinch of ajinomoto (optional)
2-3 spring onions
1 tablespoon finely chopped garlic
1 tablespoon black peppercorns, crushed
Oil for deep frying

Method:
- Peel and cut the potatoes into chips.
- Cut the spring onions into long pieces.
- Boil the potatoes in salted water for 5-7 minutes.
- Drain and set aside.

Appetisers

- Mix together the cornflour, salt, pepper and ajinomoto if using.
- Rub into the potato chips.
- Heat the oil in a karahi.
- Fry a few chips at a time until done.
- Remove all but one spoon oil from the karahi.
- Fry the spring onions, garlic, crushed peppercorns and salt over a high flame for 1 minute.
- Add the potato chips and mix well.
- Serve hot.

Cajun Oven Fried Potatoes

Ingredients:
2 tablespoons oil
2 teaspoons chilli powder
½ teaspoon dried thyme
½ teaspoon black pepper
Salt to taste
6-8 potatoes, thinly sliced

Method:
- Preheat the oven to 210°C.
- Mix the oil, chilli powder, thyme, pepper and salt into the potatoes, tossing well to coat.
- Spread out on a baking tray and bake for 40-45 minutes until brown and crisp.

Make these as spicy as you like and serve with drinks or as an after school snack.

Schezwan Potato Rolls

Ingredients:

4 potatoes, boiled
4 slices of bread crumbed
1 tablespoon chopped ginger
1 tablespoon chopped garlic
3-4 tablespoons chopped spring onions
1-2 tablespoons vinegar
Salt to taste

For the filling:
1 packet mushrooms, chopped
1-2 teaspoons sugar
3-4 tablespoons red chilly paste
2 tablespoons oil
Salt, ajinomoto to taste
Oil for deep frying

Method:
- Heat the oil and fry the garlic, ginger, spring onions along with the chilly paste.
- Add the sugar, vinegar and seasonings along with the mushrooms and stir fry over high heat until dry. Keep aside.
- Meanwhile mash the potatoes and mix in the bread and salt to taste.
- Divide the potato into 12 portions.
- Take one portion on the palm of your hand and flatten.
- Put a heaped tablespoon of the mushroom filling and fold the potato over to cover.
- Make into a roll and deep fry in hot oil until golden.
- Repeat with the remaining potato.

Potato Papad Rolls

Ingredients:

4 potatoes, boiled and peeled
1 onion, finely chopped
2 green chillies, chopped
Chopped coriander leaves
Juice of 1 lemon

8-10 papads
2 tablespoons flour
Salt and garam masala powder to taste
Oil for deep frying

Method:
- Mash the potatoes along with the onion, green chillies, coriander leaves, lemon

juice, salt and garam masala.
- Shape the potato mixture into long rolls almost the length of the papad.
- Mix the flour to a paste with water.
- Taking one papad at a time, dip in water for a few seconds.
- Place a potato roll on the corner of the papad and roll up.
- Seal the edges with the flour paste.
- Fry in hot oil until golden.
- Repeat with the remaining papads.
- Cut into pieces and serve.

Pot Roast Potatoes

Ingredients:

200 gms boiled and peeled baby potatoes
1 tablespoon oil
1 tablespoon soya sauce
2 tablespoons tomato sauce
1 tablespoon vinegar

1 teaspoon ginger garlic paste
1 teaspoon chilli powder
½ cup water
Salt to taste

Method:

- Mix all the ingredients in a karahi.
- Cover and cook on a low flame till dry.

This recipe needs absolutely no attention. Just mix all the ingredients and leave aside. Cook just before serving.

SOUPS

Mexican Chilli Potato Soup

Ingredients:

1 tablespoon oil
1 onion, chopped
1 capsicum, chopped
1 green chilli, chopped
2 cloves garlic, crushed
1 potato, peeled and cut into strips
100 gms mushrooms, sliced

½ teaspoon jeera powder
½ teaspoon dhania powder
6-8 tomatoes, peeled and chopped
Salt, pepper and sugar to taste
4 cups stock/water
Lemon juice
Lemon slices to garnish

Method:
- Heat the oil in a large saucepan and sauté the onion for 2-3 minutes.
- Add in the capsicum, green chilli, garlic and potato.
- Stir fry for 4-5 minutes.
- Add in the seasonings along with the tomatoes.
- Cook for 5-6 minutes over high heat and then add in the stock and allow to boil.
- Serve hot with lemon juice and garnished with lemon slices.

Cheesy Potato Soup

Ingredients:

2 potatoes, peeled and chopped
2 onions, chopped
1 carrot, coarsely grated
½ cup green peas
3-4 cloves garlic, crushed
2 tablespoons butter
4 cups stock
1 cup shredded cabbage
1 tablespoon cornflour dissolved in water
½ cup grated cheese
Salt and pepper to taste
Chopped parsley to garnish

Method:

- Heat the butter in a large pan and stir fry the potatoes, onion, green peas and garlic.
- Add the stock along with the salt and pepper and cook until the vegetables are done.
- Add the cabbage and carrot and continue to cook for a few minutes more.
- Thicken the soup with the cornflour dissolved in water, stirring continuously.
- Add in the grated cheese and serve hot garnished with parsley.

Warming, filling and satisfying.
Ideal for rainy or wintry evenings.

Appetisers

Potato Corn Chowder

Ingredients:

2 potatoes, peeled and chopped
1 onion, finely chopped
1 cup sweet corn
2 tablespoons flour
2 cups water
2 cups milk
1 tablespoon butter
Salt and pepper to taste
Chopped parsley to garnish

Method:

- Melt the butter in a large pan and add in the potatoes, corn and onion.
- Fry for 4-5 minutes, and add in the flour.
- Slowly add the water, stirring continuously.
- Season with salt and pepper and simmer until the vegetables are cooked.
- Pour in the milk and heat gently.
- Garnish with parsley and serve hot.

This recipe needs absolutely no attention. Just mix all the ingredients and leave aside. Cook just before serving.

Potato and Leek Soup

Ingredients:

2 leeks chopped
2-3 potatoes peeled and cubed
2 cups water
2 cups milk
1 tablespoon butter
Salt and pepper to taste
2-3 tablespoons fresh cream

Method:

- Heat the butter in a pan and sauté the potatoes and leeks for 4-5 minutes.
- Add the water and milk and simmer till the potatoes are cooked.
- Allow to cool.
- When cool, puree the soup in a blender.
- Pour back into the pan and heat gently seasoning with the salt and pepper.
- Serve hot with a dollop of cream.

A simplified version of the well known French Soup Vichyssoise. This soup can also be served chilled.

Jamaican Pepper Pot Soup

Ingredients:

1 tablespoon butter
1 onion, finely chopped
2 cloves garlic, crushed
1 potato, peeled and sliced
1 bunch spinach, washed and cut

2 green chillies
4-6 cups stock
1 cup coconut milk
Salt and pepper to taste
Extra green chilly to garnish

Method:
- Heat the butter in a large pan.
- Add the onion, garlic, potato, spinach and green chilly and stir fry.
- Add the stock, bring to a boil and allow to simmer until the vegetables are cooked.
- Blend the soup and return to the pan and boil.
- Add in the coconut milk and reheat.
- Serve hot garnished with green chillies.

This exotic soup is deliciously spicy. Reduce the chillies if you don't like so much spice.

Green Spring Soup

Ingredients:

4 potatoes, peeled and chopped
6 spring onions, chopped
1 bunch palak, chopped
1 bunch lettuce leaves, chopped
1 carrot, chopped
4 cloves garlic, crushed

4 cups stock or water
1 cup milk
1 tablespoon butter
Salt and pepper to taste
Thyme to garnish

Method:

- Heat the butter in a large pan and stir fry the potatoes, onions, palak, lettuce, carrot and garlic.
- Add the stock or water and simmer till the vegetables are cooked.
- Cool and blend.
- Return the soup to the pan and bring back to the boil, whisking in the milk, salt and pepper.
- Serve hot, garnished with thyme.

A wonderful soup. Fresh, light and full of flavour.

Country Style Potato and Lentil Soup

Ingredients:

1 tablespoon butter
1 onion, chopped
2 celery sticks, chopped
2 potatoes, peeled and cubed
½ cup yellow moong dal
3-4 cups stock
1 bay leaf
Salt and pepper to taste
Chopped parsley to garnish

Method:

- Melt the butter in a pan and add the onion, celery and potatoes and stir fry.
- Add in the lentils, stock and bay leaf, bring to the boil, cover and simmer until the potato is cooked.
- Remove the bay leaf and blend half the soup until smooth.
- Return to the pan with the remaining soup and reheat.
- Season and serve hot garnished with parsley.

A very versatile soup, substitute the moong dal with any other dal. Try red or black masoor for a change.

Potato Pesto Soup

Ingredients:

2 potatoes, peeled and diced
1 carrot, diced
1 onion, peeled and chopped
6-8 tomatoes liquidized
2 garlic cloves, crushed

½ cup soaked black eyed beans
5-6 cups water
Basil leaves
Salt and pepper to taste
1 tablespoon oil

Method:
- Fry the onion in the oil for 2-3 minutes.
- Add the potato, carrot, garlic and beans and stir fry.
- Add the tomatoes and water along with the seasoning and cook till the vegetables and beans are done, about 20-30 minutes.
- Add the basil leaves and serve hot.

This soup is a meal in itself.
All you need is garlic bread.

Spinach and Potato Soup

Ingredients:

3-4 potatoes, peeled and cubed
1 onion, finely chopped
3 cloves garlic, crushed
1 tablespoon butter
4 cups stock
1 tablespoon cornflour
1 cup milk
1 cup chopped spinach leaves
Salt and pepper to taste

Method:
- Heat the butter in a pan and stir fry the potatoes, onion and garlic.
- Add the stock and cook till the potatoes are done.
- Cool and blend the soup until smooth.
- Return to the pan, season and boil.
- Mix the cornflour with cold milk and stir into the soup stirring continuously.
- Bring to the boil again and add in the spinach leaves.
- Allow to cook for 2-3 minutes and serve hot.

Curried Potato Soup

Ingredients:

2 potatoes, peeled and chopped
2 onions, chopped
250 gm cauliflower, cut into florets
2-3 cups stock
2 tablespoons butter
1 teaspoon curry powder
1 bay leaf
2 cups coconut milk
Salt and pepper to taste
Coriander leaves
Salted peanuts, crushed
Grated coconut

Method:

- Heat the butter in a pan and add the potato, onion and cauliflower and stir fry.
- Add in the curry powder, stock, bay leaf, salt and pepper and cook until the vegetables are done.
- Cool and blend the soup.
- Return to the pan and bring to a boil.
- Stir in the coconut milk and heat.
- Serve hot garnished with coriander leaves, peanuts and grated coconut.

To make a good stock, boil together one onion, one stick celery, some lettuce leaves, some outer leaves of a cabbage along with a piece of ginger, a few whole peppers and salt to taste in 4-5 cups of water for about 20-30 minutes.

SALADS

Bean and Potato Salad

Ingredients:

1 cup soaked and cooked rajma beans
2 boiled potatoes
2 tomatoes, cut into wedges
4 spring onions, chopped
2 tablespoons chopped fresh coriander

For the dressing:

4 tablespoons oil
4 tablespoons lemon juice
½ teaspoon roasted jeera powder
Salt and pepper to taste

Method:

- Peel and cut the potatoes into cubes.
- Place the beans, potatoes, tomatoes, spring onions and coriander leaves in a bowl.
- Mix all the dressing ingredients well and pour over the vegetables.
- Toss well and chill before serving.

Rich in proteins and very colorful, this salad is a good accompaniment to almost any kind of cuisine.

Hot Potato Salad

Ingredients:

6-8 potatoes
2 onions, chopped
1 tablespoon oil
4 tablespoons white vinegar
4 tablespoons water
4 tablespoons thick dahi
2 tablespoons chopped parsley
Salt and pepper to taste

Method:

- Boil the potatoes.
- Drain and peel while still hot.
- Cut into thin slices and place in a serving dish.
- Stir fry the onions in the oil until transparent.
- Gently pour in the vinegar and water.
- Bring to a boil and remove from the heat.
- Stir in the thick dahi and season to taste with the salt and pepper.
- Pour this dressing over the potatoes.
- Sprinkle with parsley and serve.

The trick in making this salad is to put the still warm potatoes into the sharp dressing.

German Potato Salad

Ingredients:

4 potatoes, boiled and cubed
1 onion, finely chopped
1 capsicum, finely chopped
1 stalk celery, finely chopped
2 eggs, boiled and sliced
½ cup water
1/3 cup vinegar
1 tablespoon sugar
2 teaspoons flour
Salt and pepper to taste
Parsley to garnish

Method:

- Mix the potatoes, onion, capsicum and celery in a bowl.
- Mix the water, vinegar, sugar, flour, salt and pepper in a pan.
- Whisk well and bring to a boil over moderate heat.
- Pour this hot dressing over the vegetables in the bowl.
- Cool and top with the eggs and parsley.
- Chill well before serving.

Pouring the hot dressing over the potato salad allows the potatoes to absorb the flavour of the dressing.

Black and White Salad

Ingredients:

4-5 boiled potatoes
2 tomatoes
3 spring onions
½ cup black olives

4-6 tablespoons thick dahi
2 tablespoons milk
Salt and pepper to taste

Method:
- Peel and dice the potatoes.
- Chop the spring onions and the tomatoes.
- Mix all the vegetables together along with the olives and add in the dahi, milk and seasoning.
- Mix well and chill before serving.

Hawaiian Potato Salad

Ingredients:
4 potatoes, boiled and cubed
1 cup corn, boiled
4-5 slices pineapple, cubed
1 capsicum, cut into strips
2 tomatoes, cut into wedges
For the dressing:
4 tablespoons honey

4 tablespoons oil
4 tablespoons lemon juice
½ teaspoon mustard powder
Salt and pepper to taste

Method:
- Mix the potatoes, corn, pineapple and capsicum in a bowl.
- Mix the ingredients for the dressing and pour over.
- Toss the salad and garnish with tomato wedges before serving.

Swedish Potato Salad

Ingredients:

4-5 boiled potatoes
2 cooked beetroots
1 cucumber
5-6 tablespoons mayonnaise
1 clove finely chopped garlic
Salt and pepper to taste
1 tablespoon chopped dill
Extra dill leaves for garnishing

Method:
- Peel and dice the potatoes.
- Peel and chop the beetroot and the cucumber.
- Mix the mayonnaise, garlic and dill along with the seasonings.
- Add in the prepared vegetables and mix well.
- Chill the salad and garnish with dill before serving.

Dill or Suva as this vegetable is locally known, gives a lovely flavour to the salad. If unavailable, substitute with parsley or coriander leaves.

Potato and Sweet Potato Salad with Ginger Orange Dressing

Ingredients:

2 potatoes, boiled and cubed
2 sweet potatoes, boiled and cubed
2 sticks celery, chopped
4 spring onions, chopped
Shredded red cabbage

For the dressing:
¼ cup orange juice
1 teaspoon grated fresh ginger
1 tablespoon honey
1 tablespoon white vinegar
1 teaspoon grated orange rind

Method:

- Mix the potatoes, sweet potatoes, celery and spring onions in a bowl.
- Mix all the ingredients for the dressing and toss into the salad.
- Serve chilled garnished with shredded red cabbage.

Sweet and sour and tangy - and absolutely delicious is how I would describe this salad.

Creamy Minted Potato

Ingredients:

2 potatoes, boiled and cubed
2 cucumbers, peeled and cubed
1 capsicum, finely chopped
4 cups dahi
Mint leaves, finely chopped

1 tablespoon oil
1 teaspoon jeera seeds
½ teaspoon chilly powder
½ teaspoon black salt
Salt to taste

Method:
- Whisk the dahi and mix in the vegetables.
- Heat the oil in a pan and splutter the jeera seeds.
- Pour this over the dahi and mix well adding salt along with the other masalas and mint leaves.
- Chill well before serving garnished with extra chopped mint leaves.

Very refreshing-you can also serve this as a raita along with stuffed parathas or a pulao.

Salads

Mediterranean Potato Platter

Ingredients:

4 potatoes, boiled and peeled
1 onion, finely chopped
1 capsicum, finely chopped
1 red capsicum, finely chopped
Parsley, chopped
Stuffed olives, sliced

For the dressing:
4 tablespoons oil
4 tablespoons white vinegar
2 cloves garlic, crushed
½ teaspoon mustard powder
½ teaspoon dried oregano
½ teaspoon sugar
Salt and pepper to taste

Method:
- Slice the potatoes and lay onto a salad platter.
- Combine the onion and capsicums and sprinkle over the potato slices.
- For the dressing, combine all the ingredients in a bottle with a tight fitting lid and shake well.
- Pour over the salad platter.
- Garnish with the parsley and the olives and chill before serving.

Potato Waldorf Salad

Ingredients:

2 boiled potatoes
2 red apples
2 celery sticks
$\frac{1}{2}$ cup chopped walnuts
6-8 tablespoons mayonnaise
Lettuce leaves for serving

Method:

- Peel and cut the potatoes into cubes.
- Core and cut the apple into similar size cubes.
- Chop the celery.
- Mix all the ingredients and chill well.
- Serve on a bed of lettuce leaves.

The addition of potatoes to the popular Waldorf Salad makes an interesting change.

RICE AND ROTIS

Kashmiri Aloo Pulao

Ingredients:

2 cups rice
2 potatoes, peeled and cubed
½ teaspoon shahjeera
1 stick dalchini
4 lavangs

2 bay leaves
1 cup milk
Oil for deep frying
1 can fruit cocktail, drained
Salt to taste

Method:
- Wash and soak the rice and keep aside.
- Heat the oil and deep fry the potato cubes until light brown and keep aside.
- Remove all but 2 tablespoons oil from the pan and add the shahjeera, dalchini, lavang and bay leaf.
- Add the rice along with the milk, salt and 3 cups of water and boil.
- Cover and cook until the rice is ¾ th done.
- Toss in the fried potato cubes and fruit.
- Cover and allow to cook for a few minutes more.
- Serve hot.

Aloo Masala Bhaat

Ingredients:
2-3 potatoes
½ cup green peas
1 teaspoon jeera,
whole garam masala
(kaali mirchi, lavang, dalchini)
2 cups rice washed and soaked in water
¼ teaspoon haldi
1 teaspoon dhania powder
¼ teaspoon jeera powder
2 tablespoons oil
¼ teaspoon garam masala
Salt to taste

For the masala:
4 tablespoons grated coconut
4 tablespoons coriander leaves
4-5 green chillies
1 teaspoon garlic paste
1 teaspoon ginger paste
2 chopped onions
For the garnish:
Cashewnuts

Method:
- Cut the potatoes into bite size pieces.
- Grind all the ingredients for the masala to a paste in a mixer.
- Heat the oil in a pan and add jeera and whole garam masalas.
- Add the ground masala paste and fry till the oil seperates.
- Add the haldi, dhania, jeera powder and garam masala powders and fry for a minute more.
- Now put in the rice and vegetables and mix till the masala coats the vegetables.
- Add in four cups of water and salt.
- When the liquid comes to a boil, lower the heat, cover and cook for 12-15 minutes or till the rice is cooked.
- Garnish with cashewnuts and serve.

Aloo Biryani

Ingredients:

2 potatoes, peeled and cubed
2 cups mixed vegetables
2 cups rice
2 onions, sliced
1 cup dahi
3-4 tablespoons oil
Salt to taste
½ teaspoon saffron
¼ cup milk
For the masala:
8-10 cloves garlic
1 inch piece ginger
2 green chillies
1 teaspoon garam masala
8-10 cashewnuts
1 cup coriander leaves
Few mint leaves
1 teaspoon cumin seeds
1 teaspoon chilly powder
1 teaspoon coriander
Crisp fried onions

Method:

- Cook the rice till ¾ th done and keep aside.
- Heat the oil in a pan and stir fry the onions till brown.
- Grind all the ingredients for the masala.
- Add the masala paste to the fried onions and fry for 4-5 minutes more.
- Add the dahi along with the vegetables and salt.
- Cover and cook until the vegetables are done.
- Spread ½ the rice in a large pan.
- Top with the vegetable mix.
- Cover the vegetables with the remaining rice.
- Mix the saffron in the milk and sprinkle over.
- Cover the biryani with a tight fitting lid and cook on dum.
- Garnish with fried onions.

Rice and Rotis

Potato and Tomato Rice

Ingredients:

2 cups rice
2 cups tomato puree
2 carrots, grated
2 potatoes
2 onions, sliced
1 capsicum, cut into strips

1 teaspoon jeera
2 bay leaves
1 teaspoon chilly powder
1 teaspoon sugar
Salt to taste
2 tablespoons oil

Method:
- Wash and soak the rice the rice.
- Peel and cut the potatoes into strips.
- Heat the oil in a pan and stir fry the potato strips until brown.
- Remove and keep aside.
- In the same pan stir fry the onions until golden.
- Add the jeera and allow the seeds to brown.
- Mix in the capsicum and carrot and fry for 3-4 minutes.
- Drain the rice and add in.
- Stir fry and add the potatoes, tomato puree, bay leaves, chilly powder, sugar and salt to taste.
- Stir once and add 2 cups of water and boil.
- Lower the heat, cover the pan with a lid and cook until the liquid is absorbed and the rice is cooked.

To make fresh tomato puree, cook 4-6 tomatoes with just the water clinging to them. Cool and blend in a mixie then cook for about 5-7 minutes.

Green Aloo Pulao

Ingredients:

10-12 small potatoes, peeled
2 cups rice
2 onions, chopped
2 sticks dalchini
3-4 lavang
2 big elaichis
1 tej patta
3-4 tablespoons oil
Salt to taste

For the masala paste:
1 bunch coriander leaves
6-8 green chillies
8-10 cloves garlic
2-3 tablespoons grated coconut

Method:
- Wash and soak the rice.
- Grind all the ingredients for the masala to a smooth paste.
- Heat the oil in a pan and add in the dalchini, lavang, elaichi and tej patta along with the onions.
- Fry for about 4-5 minutes and add in the masala paste.
- Fry for 4-5 minutes more.
- Add the rice, potatoes, salt and 4 cups of water and bring to a boil.
- Cover and simmer until the rice is cooked. Serve hot.

Minty Potato Pulao

Ingredients:

2 potatoes, peeled and cubed
2 cups rice
2 onions, sliced
2 sticks dalchini
3-4 lavang
2 big elaichis
1 tej patta
1 cup mint leaves
2 teaspoons saunf
3-4 tablespoons oil
Salt to taste

Method:
- Wash and soak the rice.
- Boil 4 cups of water with mint leaves and saunf for 5 minutes and strain.

- Heat the oil in a pan and add in the dalchini, lavang, elaichi and tej patta along with the onions.
- Fry for about 4-5 minutes until the onions brown.
- Add the rice, potatoes, salt and strained mint liquid and bring to a boil.
- Cover and simmer until the rice is cooked.
- Serve hot.

Potato Puris

Ingredients:

3-4 potatoes, boiled
½ cup grated coconut
½ cup roasted peanuts, crushed
3-4 green chillies, chopped
1 tablespoon ginger, grated
Salt to taste
2 cups atta
Oil for deep frying

Method:

- Mash the potatoes and mix in the coconut, peanuts, green chillies, ginger and salt to taste.
- Divide into 12 portions.
- Knead the atta adding salt to taste into a soft dough.
- Take a portion of the atta and flatten.
- Put a portion of the potato mixture and cover with the dough.
- Make into a ball and roll out using extra flour.
- Repeat with the remaining dough and filling.
- Deep fry in hot oil until well risen and golden.
- Serve hot.

Potato and Cheese Parathas

Ingredients:

3-4 potatoes, peeled and chopped
4 green chillies, chopped
1 inch piece ginger, grated
1 teaspoon jeera
4-6 tablespoons grated cheese
Salt to taste
2 cups wheat flour
Oil or ghee for shallow frying

Method:

- Heat 1 tablespoon of oil in a karahi and add the jeera.
- When the seeds splutter, add in the potatoes, green chillies and ginger.
- Add salt to taste and cover and cook until the potatoes are soft.
- Meanwhile make the dough adding salt to taste and water to the flour.
- Knead well and divide into 10-12 portions.
- When the potatoes are done add the cheese and mash the mixture well.
- To prepare the parathas, take each portion of the dough and roll into a circle about 6-7 inches in diameter.
- Take a portion of the filling and spread on one round of dough.
- Cover with another circle and press down, sealing the edges well.
- Place this stuffed paratha on a heated tava and allow to cook.
- Turn over and cook the other side.
- Smear with teaspoons of ghee or oil.
- Repeat with the remaining dough.
- Serve hot.

For a tangy raita to go with parathas add a finely chopped banana, apple and cucumber to 2 cups dahi. Season with salt, sugar and jeera powder.

Aloo Gobhi Paratha

Ingredients:

4 potatoes, boiled
1 cup gobhi, grated
2 green chillies, chopped
1 inch piece ginger, grated
4 tablespoons chopped coriander leaves

½ teaspoon jeera powder
½ teaspoon ajwain
Salt to taste
2 cups atta
Ghee or oil for frying

Method:
- Mix the atta with just enough water to make a soft dough.
- Mash the potatoes and mix the gobhi, chillies, ginger, coriander, jeera, ajwain and salt.
- Divide into 8 portions.
- Take a ball of dough and flatten.
- Put a portion of the vegetable filling and cover pulling the dough over.
- Roll and make into a ball.
- Flatten and roll into a paratha using extra flour as needed.
- Fry gently on a hot tava using a teaspoon or two of ghee until golden.
- Repeat with the remaining dough and filling. Serve hot.

Rice and Rotis

INDIAN MAIN COURSE

Aloo Papad Mangodi

Ingredients:

2 potatoes, peeled and cut into small cubes
½ cup mangodi (small moong dal wadis)
2 small papads, cut into pieces
½ teaspoon jeera
¼ teaspoon hing
½ teaspoon chilly powder
¼ teaspoon haldi powder
½ teaspoon ginger powder
½ teaspoon besan
1 cup dahi
2 tablespoons oil
Garam masala and coriander leaves to garnish

Method:

- Heat one tablespoon oil in a pan and stir fry the mangodis until brown.
- Remove and keep aside.
- Heat the remaining oil in the same pan and add jeera.
- When the jeera splutters, add the hing, chilly powder, haldi and ginger.
- Immediately add the potatoes, papad pieces and mangodis.
- Add half a cup of water along with salt to taste and cook until the potatoes are done.
- Meanwhile mix the besan and dahi and add into the potato gravy.
- Simmer and serve hot garnished with garam masala and chopped coriander leaves.

Potato Dum Pukht

Ingredients:

10-12 small potatoes, peeled
2 onions
10 almonds, peeled
15-20 raisins
4 green elaichis
4 lavangs
Small piece of dalchini

1 pinch of kesar soaked in milk
1 teaspoon ginger paste
4-5 kashmiri chillies
2 cups dahi
Salt to taste
Oil for deep frying
Fresh cream for garnishing

Method:

- Heat the oil for deep frying.
- Slice one onion finely and deep fry till brown.
- Drain and keep aside.
- Fry the potatoes in the same oil until light brown.
- Grind the remaining onion, almonds, raisins, elaichi, lavang, dalchini, kesar, ginger and kashmiri chillies to a smooth paste.
- Beat the dahi into this ground masala paste.
- Heat 2 tablespoons oil in a pan with a tight fitting lid and add the dahi mixture along with the potatoes and salt to taste.
- Mix well and close the lid tight.
- Alternately, seal the pan with atta dough and place on a tava on a low flame for 30-40 minutes.
- Open the lid and garnish with fried onion and cream before serving.

Moghlai Aloo

Ingredients:

8-10 medium potatoes, peeled
10 almonds
10 cashewnuts
1 tablespoon khus khus
1 inch piece ginger
4 green chillies
½ bunch coriander leaves
1 teaspoon dhania powder
1 teaspoon jeera powder
1 teaspoon garam masala
2 cups thick dahi
Salt to taste
Oil for deep frying
¼ teaspoon saffron
1 tablespoon milk
Fresh cream to garnish

Method:
- Prick the potatoes with a needle or a fork and deep fry in hot oil until golden.
- Drain and keep aside.
- Grind the almonds, cashewnuts, khus khus, ginger, green chillies and coriander leaves to a paste.
- Remove all but 2 tablespoons oil from the karahi and fry the paste along with the dhania, jeera and garam masala powders.
- Add the dahi and cook over a medium fire until the gravy begins to boil.
- Add the fried potatoes along with the salt adding water as needed, and cook until the potatoes are well done.
- Dissolve the saffron in milk and pour over along with the cream to garnish.

Hyderabadi Aloo

Ingredients:

15-20 small potatoes, peeled
½ teaspoon rye
8-10 curry leaves
2 onions, grated
¼ teaspoon haldi
1 tablespoon tamarind paste
Oil for deep frying

1 tablespoon dhania seeds
2 tablespoons til seeds
1 teaspoon jeera
3-4 dry kashmiri chillies
6-8 cloves garlic
1 inch piece ginger

For the masala:
½ cup roasted peanuts

Method:
- Heat the oil in a karahi and deep fry the potatoes until golden brown.
- Drain and keep aside.
- Grind the ingredients for the masala using a little water to a fine paste.
- Remove all but 3 tablespoons of the oil from the karahi and add the mustard seeds.
- When the seeds crackle, add in the onions along with the curry leaves and fry until light golden.
- Add the masala paste and fry until the raw smell disappears.
- Stir in the haldi, tamarind paste, 2 cups water and salt to taste along with the potatoes.
- Bring to a boil, cover and simmer until the potatoes are cooked.
- Serve hot.

Kerala Potato Stew

Ingredients:

4 potatoes, peeled and cubed
4-5 lavangs
4 green elaichis
Small piece of dalchini
2 onions, thinly sliced
1 tablespoon ginger, chopped
1 tablespoon garlic, chopped
3-4 green chillies, slit
7-8 curry leaves
1 tablespoon rice flour
2 cups coconut milk
Salt to taste
2 tablespoons oil

Method:
- Heat the ghee in a pan and splutter the lavang, elaichi and dalchini.
- Add in the onions, ginger, garlic and green chilly and stir fry until pink.
- Add in the rice flour, potato cubes, curry leaves and salt along with a cup of water and cook.
- When the potatoes are almost done, add in the curry leaves.
- Add the coconut milk and boil once before serving hot.

Aloo Posto

Ingredients:

4-5 potatoes, peeled and cubed
½ teaspoon jeera
2-3 tablespoons khus khus
2 green chillies
Small bit of ginger
1 tablespoon oil
Salt to taste
Red chilly powder to garnish

Method:
- Soak the jeera and khus khus in ½ cup warm water for about 2-3 hours.
- Grind to a paste along with the green chilly and ginger.
- Warm the oil in a karahi and add the potatoes and salt to taste.
- Cover and cook for 5-7 minutes until the potatoes are semi cooked.
- Add the khus khus paste and stir.

- Cover and allow to simmer till the potatoes are cooked adding more water if needed.
- Garnish with a sprinkling of red chilly powder.

Aloo Kurma

Ingredients:

4 potatoes, peeled and cubed
1 onion, thinly sliced
2 green chillies, slit
4-6 tablespoons grated coconut
1 teaspoon saunf
3 lavangs
3 green elaichis
Small piece dalchini

2 teaspoons ginger garlic paste
$\frac{1}{2}$ teaspoon chilli powder
1 teaspoon dhania powder
2 tablespoons oil
Salt to taste
Chopped coriander leaves to garnish

Method:

- Heat the oil in a pan and fry the onion and green chillies till the onions brown.
- Add the ginger garlic paste and stir fry.
- Add the potato cubes, chilli and dhania powders.
- Fry for a few minutes more and add one cup of water and salt to taste.
- Simmer till the potatoes are cooked.
- Meanwhile, grind together the coconut, saunf, lavang, elaichi and dalchini to a smooth paste.
- Add this masala paste to the cooked potatoes along with a little masala and boil.
- Garnish with fresh coriander leaves and serve hot.

Aloo Kofta in Mattar Gravy

Ingredients:

2 potatoes, boiled
2 tablespoons flour
Salt to taste

For the filling:
1 cup mixed vegetables, boiled
1 tablespoon coriander leaves, chopped
2-3 green chillies, chopped
½ teaspoon garam masala powder
Salt to taste

For the gravy:
2 onions, chopped
2 cups green peas
2 teaspoons ginger garlic paste
1 teaspoon dhania powder
1 teaspoon chilly powder
2 tablespoon chopped cashewnuts
Salt to taste
Oil for deep frying

Method:

For the koftas:

- Heat the oil for deep frying in a karahi.
- Mash the potatoes and knead in the flour, adding salt to taste.
- Mix all the ingredients for the filling.
- Divide the potato mixture into 8 portions.
- Flatten each portion and place a heaped tablespoon of the filling on the potato circle.
- Shape into round balls and deep fry in hot oil.

For the gravy:

- Remove all but 2 tablespoons oil from the karahi and fry the onion until soft.
- Add the ginger garlic paste, dhania and chilly powder and fry.
- Add the peas and cashewnuts along with a cup of water and salt to taste and simmer for 4-5 minutes till the peas are cooked.
- Let this masala cool a bit and then blend in a mixer.
- Return to the karahi and bring to a boil adding more water if needed.
- Put in the koftas, boil again and serve hot.

Aloo Mattar Kheema

Ingredients:

4 potatoes, peeled and cut into small cubes
2 onions, finely chopped
2 tomatoes, finely chopped
2 teaspoons ginger garlic paste
1 teaspoon chilly powder
2 teaspoons coriander powder
½ teaspoon haldi powder
1 teaspoon garam masala powder
1 cup green peas
Salt to taste
Oil for deep frying
Coriander leaves for garnishing

Method:
- Heat the oil in a karahi and deep fry the potato cubes, and keep aside.
- Remove all but 2 tablespoons oil from the karahi and stir fry the onions over a low flame until soft.
- Add the ginger garlic paste and fry for 4-5 minutes more.
- Add the tomatoes along with the chilly powder, coriander, haldi and garam masala and fry till the oil separates.
- Add the peas and fried potatoes along with the salt and mix.
- Pour in 1½ cups water, cover and cook until the peas are tender.
- Garnish with coriander leaves and serve hot.

For a tasty and healthy variation, add ½ a cup of soaked soya granules along with the peas and fried potatoes.

Indian Main Course

Aloo Do Pyaza

Ingredients:

2-3 potatoes, peeled and cubed
250 gms mixed vegetables, diced
2-3 tomatoes, cut into big pieces
2 onions, cut into big pieces

For the masala:
2 onions, thinly sliced
2 teaspoons ginger garlic paste
$\frac{1}{2}$ teaspoon chilly powder
$\frac{1}{4}$ teaspoon haldi
2 teaspoons dhania powder
1 teaspoon jeera powder
$\frac{1}{2}$ cup dahi
2-3 tablespoons oil
$\frac{1}{2}$ teaspoon garam masala
Salt to taste
Green chillies to garnish

Method:
- Heat the oil in a karahi and fry the thinly sliced onions until golden.
- Add the ginger garlic paste, chilly, haldi, dhania and jeera powder and fry till the oil separates.
- Add the vegetables along with salt to taste and mix well.
- Add the dahi and half a cup of water and simmer on a low flame until the potatoes are cooked.
- Sprinkle the garam masala and serve hot garnished with green chillies.

To make a Chicken Do Pyaaza, substitute the vegetables with 250 gms of boneless diced chicken. Add the chicken along with the potatoes and cook until tender.

Indian Main Course

Khatte Aloo

Ingredients:

4-6 potatoes, boiled and cubed
4 tablespoons anardana
4 tablespoons jeera
1 tablespoon dhania powder
1 teaspoon chilly powder
1 teaspoon garam masala
1 teaspoon kala namak
2 tablespoons oil
Salt to taste
Onion rings and lemon slices to garnish

Method:

- Dry roast the anardana and jeera until brown and fragrant.
- Cool and powder in a grinder.
- Heat the oil in a karahi and add in the powdered masala along with all the dry masalas and stir fry.
- Add the potatoes along with salt to taste and cook over a slow fire tossing well to coat the potatoes with the masala.
- Serve hot garnished with onion rings and lemon slices.

Goan Potato Curry

Ingredients:

4 potatoes, cut into big pieces
1 onion, sliced
½ coconut, grated
1 tablespoon dhania seeds
1 teaspoon jeera
1 stick dalchini
2-3 lavang
2-3 whole kali mirchi
6-8 cloves garlic
8-10 dried kashmiri chillies
2 large tomatoes
1 tablespoon oil
Salt to taste

Method:

- Heat the oil in a pan and add the onion, coconut, dhania, jeera, dalchini, lavang, kali mirchi, garlic and kashmiri chillies.
- Fry for about 8-10 minutes.
- Cool and grind the masala paste in a mixer.
- Put the masala paste back into the pan and continue frying till the oil separates.
- Liquidise the tomatoes and add to the masala and cook.
- Add in the potato pieces along with 2-3 cups of water and salt to taste and cook, covered until the potatoes are done.
- Serve hot with boiled rice.

Red Hot Potatoes

Ingredients:

5-6 potatoes
7-8 dry kashmiri chillies
2 tablespoons jeera
8-10 cloves garlic
2 tablespoons tamarind paste
8-10 curry leaves
3-4 tablespoons oil
Salt to taste
Coriander leaves and lemon to garnish

Method:
- Boil the potatoes.
- Peel and cut into cubes.
- Soak the chillies and tamarind seperately in warm water for 15-20 minutes while the potatoes are cooking.
- Grind together the chillies, garlic and jeera to a fine paste.
- Heat the oil in a pan and add the curry leaves and the masala paste.
- Fry till the oil separates.
- Add the potatoes, the tamarind paste along with a little water to the masala.
- Add salt to taste and mix well.
- Simmer for 3-4 minutes and serve hot garnished with coriander leaves.

To make tamarind paste for storing, clean and soak about 250 gms tamarind. Blend and sieve the paste. Boil this paste along with a little salt until thick. Store for 3-4 weeks in the fridge.

Quick and Easy Potato Curry

Ingredients:

4 potatoes, peeled and cubed
1 onion, peeled and cut
2 tomatoes, cut
4-5 cloves garlic
Small bit of ginger
2 green chillies
Coriander leaves

Few mint leaves
$\frac{1}{2}$ teaspoon chilly powder
$\frac{1}{2}$ teaspoon haldi powder
2 teaspoons coriander powder
Salt to taste
2 tablespoons oil

Method:

- Put the onion, tomatoes, garlic, ginger, green chillies, coriander and mint leaves in a mixer and blend until smooth.
- Heat the oil in a pan and pour the masala paste in.
- Stir fry, stirring often until the oil separates.
- Add the potatoes, along with the chilly powder, haldi, coriander, salt and 3-4 cups water.
- Bring to a boil, cover and simmer until the potatoes are cooked.

This is a wonderful recipe for just about any curry. Try it with fish. When the masala fries, add the water first. When the curry comes to a boil, add the fish slices and cook until done.

Indian Main Course

Shahi Aloo Bharta

Ingredients:

4 potatoes, boiled
1 tablespoon oil
1 teaspoon jeera
2 onions, chopped
2 green chillies, chopped
Salt and garam masala powder to taste
Coriander leaves, chopped
A piece of coal
1 teaspoon ghee

Method:

- Peel and mash the potatoes coarsely.
- Heat the oil in a karahi and add the jeera.
- Add in the onion and green chilly and stir fry for about 4-5 minutes.
- Add the mashed potatoes along with the seasoning and heat through.
- Meanwhile, heat the coal over an open fire, using a pair of tongs.
- When the coal is red hot, place it in a heatproof container and place the container in the Bharta.
- Put the ghee on the hot coal and cover the karahi to seal in the smoke which gives a lovely flavor to the bharta.
- Serve hot.

Indian Main Course

Tilwale Aloo

Ingredients:

4-5 potatoes
1 teaspoon jeera
2 tablespoons sesame seeds
2-3 slit green clillies
12 curry leaves
1 teaspoon chilly powder
½ teaspoon haldi powder
½ teaspoon sugar
Salt to taste
Coriander leaves to garnish
Oil for deep frying

Method:
- Peel and cut the potatoes into chips.
- Heat the oil and deep fry till golden.
- Drain the chips well and keep aside.
- Remove the oil from the pan.
- Take about a teaspoon of the oil and add the jeera and sesame seeds.
- Roast till the seeds splutter and add in the green chillies and the curry leaves.
- Now add the fried potato chips along with all the seasonings.
- Stir fry over a high flame for 2-3 minutes.
- Garnish with coriander leaves before serving.

Indian Main Course

Sponge Curry

Ingredients:

16 small potatoes
½ cup milk
1 stick dalchini
3-4 elaichis
6 lavangs
1 lemon
2 tablespoons oil

Salt to taste
1 onion
6 cloves garlic
Small piece ginger
1 teaspoon haldi
1 teaspoon chilli powder

Method:
- Peel the potatoes and prick them well using a fork or skewer.
- Soak the potatoes in cold water for 10-15 minutes.
- Grind the onion, garlic, ginger haldi and chilly powder to a fine paste.
- Drain off the water from the potatoes and mix in the masala paste, salt, milk and lemon juice.
- Allow the potatoes to marinate in this mixture for about an hour.
- Heat the oil in a pan and fry the dalchini, elaichi and lavang.
- Put in the potatoes along with salt to taste.
- Cover and cook over a low fire until the potatoes are cooked.

Cook this dish on a very low flame as there is no added water, preferably just before serving to avoid reheating. The potatoes can be left marinated for a longer time if needed.

Indian Main Course

INTERNATIONAL MAIN COURSE

Potato Gnocchi

Ingredients:
6-8 potatoes, boiled
2-3 tablespoons butter
1 egg
2 cups flour
Salt to taste

For the sauce:
4 tablespoons olive oil
2 cloves garlic, crushed
Mixed herbs

Method:
- Peel and mash the potatoes whilst hot.
- Add butter, egg, salt and 1 ½ cups flour and mix well.
- Turn the mixture onto a lightly floured surface and knead adding the remaining flour until a smooth dough is formed.
- Make small rolls of the dough using extra flour.
- Boil a large pan of salted water and add the gnocchi a few at a time removing them as they come to the surface.
- Cook all the gnocchi in the same way.
- For serving, warm the oil in a pan and stir fry the garlic.
- Add the gnocchi along with the seasonings and toss to coat.
- Serve immediately.

Potato Florentine

Ingredients:

4 potatoes, boiled
4 bundles palak
2 tablespoons butter
1 onion, chopped
2-3 green chillies, chopped
1 tablespoon flour

For the White Sauce:
2 tablespoons butter
2 tablespoons flour
3 cups milk
4 tablespoons grated cheese
Salt and pepper to taste

Method:

- Wash and cook the palak without adding any water.
- Cool and blend.
- Heat the butter and stir fry the onion and green chilly.
- Add the flour and mix.
- Add in the ground palak, season with salt and pepper and boil.
- Remove and spread in an ovenproof dish.
- Peel and slice the potatoes and lay the slices over the palak in the dish.
- To prepare the sauce, melt the butter in a pan and add the flour.
- Stir fry and remove from heat.
- Gradually add in the milk, stirring well.
- Return to heat and cook until the sauce thickens.
- Season to taste with salt and pepper and pour over the potatoes.
- Sprinkle the cheese over the sauce and grill or bake in a hot oven until the cheese melts.
- Serve hot.

Patatas Bravas-Spanish Potatoes

Ingredients:

4-5 potatoes peeled and cut into cubes
4-5 tablespoons oil
3 onions chopped
8-10 cloves garlic chopped
1 tablespoon maida
8-10 tomatoes liquidized
½ cup wine (optional)
Salt, pepper, chilli powder to taste

Method:
- Heat 3 tablespoons of the oil in a karahi and fry the potatoes till cooked and golden.
- Sprinkle salt and leave aside.
- To prepare the sauce, heat the remaining oil and fry the onions and garlic till light brown.
- Add the flour and stir well.
- Add the tomato, wine if using, and the seasoning and allow to boil for about 15 minutes till thick.
- Keep the pan covered lightly to avoid the tomatoes from spluttering.
- Pour the hot sauce over the potatoes and serve.

Creole Potatoes

Ingredients:

4-6 potatoes, boiled
3-4 tablespoons butter
2 onions, finely chopped
3-4 tablespoons tomato sauce
1 teaspoon mustard
1 teaspoon chilly sauce
Salt and pepper to taste

Method:
- Cut the potatoes into thick slices.
- Heat the butter in a frying pan and stir fry the onion for 6-8 minutes until soft.
- Add the sliced potatoes and continue cooking until the potatoes are lightly browned.

- Mix together the tomato sauce, mustard and chilly sauce along with the salt and pepper and pour over the potatoes.
- Heat and serve.

Potato and Onion Casserole

Ingredients:

3-4 potatoes, peeled and thinly sliced
2 onions, peeled and sliced
4-6 tablespoons grated cheese
2 cups milk
Salt and pepper to taste
50 grams butter

Method:

- Set the oven to 180°C.
- Grease a ovenproof baking dish with a little butter.
- Arrange layers of potato and onion sprinkling each layer with salt, pepper and grated cheese.
- Pour the milk over and dot with the remaining butter.
- Bake for 1 hour or until the potatoes are cooked.

The simplest of dishes made with potatoes, this goes very well with any chicken dish.

Kung Pao Potatoes

Ingredients:

4 potatoes, peeled and cut into chips
7-8 dry red chillies
2 tablespoon chopped garlic
2 tablespoons chopped ginger
3-4 spring onions, cut into long pieces
2 tablespoon soy sauce
2 tablespoons vinegar

1 tablespoon sugar
1 cup vegetable stock or water
1 tablespoon cornflour
Oil for deep frying
Salt to taste
Fried cashewnuts to garnish

Method:

- Heat the oil in a karahi and deep fry the chips until golden.
- Drain and keep aside. Remove all but 1 tablespoon oil from the karahi.
- Add the chillies, ginger and garlic and fry for a minute or two.
- Add the potatoes, soy sauce, vinegar, sugar, stock and salt to taste.
- Thicken the sauce with the cornflour dissolved in water.
- Add the spring onions and simmer.
- Garnish with fried cashewnuts and serve hot.

Roast Potatoes

Ingredients:
6-8 potatoes, peeled and cut into large pieces
4-6 tablespoons oil
Salt to taste

Method:
- Cook the potatoes in a pan of salted boiling water for 10 minutes and drain.
- Preheat the oven to 180°C.
- Place the potatoes in a baking pan with the hot oil and bake for 1 hour or until the potatoes are golden brown, basting from time to time with the oil.
- Sprinkle with salt and serve hot.

To make parsley potatoes, toss the potatoes after cooking with 3-4 tablespoons of chopped parsley leaves along with the salt.

International Main Course

Potato and Cauliflower Goulash

Ingredients:

3-4 potatoes cut into cubes
2 onions, sliced
1 cauliflower cut into florets
1 capsicum diced
100 gm mushrooms quartered
1 tablespoon wheat flour

Salt and pepper to taste
1 cup vegetable stock
1 cup low fat dahi
4-5 tomatoes liquidised
1 tablespoon oil
Chopped parsley

Method:
- Heat the oil in a pan and fry the onions and capsicum until soft.
- Add the flour and cook for a minute more.
- Add the tomato puree and stir again as the mixture thickens.
- Add the remaining vegetables and stock, seasoning lightly with salt and pepper.
- Cook on a low flame, covered, until the vegetables are tender.
- While serving, stir in the dahi and sprinkle with parsley.

Serve this goulash with warm, crusty bread, or else serve it with pasta lightly tossed in crushed garlic and olive oil. A fresh green salad completes the meal.

Potato and Mushroom Au Gratin

Ingredients:
4 large potatoes, peeled and cut into cubes
200 grams mushrooms, sliced
4 cups milk
3 tablespoons flour
50 grams butter
Salt and pepper to taste
Sliced tomatoes for garnishing

Method:
- Boil the potatoes with salt to taste until tender.
- Drain and put in an ovenproof dish.
- Meanwhile, melt the butter in a pan and fry the mushrooms for about 2-3 minutes.
- Add the flour and mix well.
- Add in the milk and stir over the heat until thick.
- Simmer for a few minutes and season with salt and pepper.
- Pour over the potatoes, decorate with sliced tomatoes and grill for a few minutes before serving.

International Main Course

Chilly Garlic Potatoes

Ingredients:

4-6 potatoes cut into fingers
1 tablespoon chopped garlic
1 tablespoon chopped ginger
1 tablespoon red chilli paste
½ cup tomato sauce

Spring onion leaves
1 tablespoon oil
1 cup stock
1 tablespoon cornflour dissolved in water

Method:

- Heat the oil and add in the garlic and ginger.
- Stir fry and add in the red chilli paste.
- Fry and add the tomato sauce and stock and boil.
- Thicken with cornflour and add in the potatoes and spring onions.
- Mix well and serve hot.

Vegetable Hakka Noodles make a good accompaniment to this potato dish.

Potato Cheese Pie

Ingredients:

6-8 potatoes, boiled
1 tablespoon butter
Salt and pepper to taste
Milk to mix
Cheese filling:
1 tablespoon butter

1 tablespoon flour
1½ cups milk
Salt and pepper to taste
100 gms cheese, grated
Parsley to garnish

Method:
- Peel the potatoes whilst still hot and mash.
- Beat in the butter and seasoning.
- Add sufficient milk to make a creamy mixture.
- Line an ovenproof dish with the mashed potato mixture and grill until golden brown.
- Meanwhile make the filling.
- Whisk the flour, milk and butter and heat over a high flame stirring continuously until thick.
- Season to taste and add in the grated cheese.
- Pour the filling into the potato pie and serve hot, or prepare earlier and bake in a preheated oven for 10-15 minutes before serving.
- Garnish with parsley before serving.

For a party, top the pie with sliced mushrooms, red and green capsicums and sliced tomatoes. Bake before serving.

Deluxe Potato Bake

Ingredients:

3-4 potatoes, grated
2 spring onions, chopped
4 slices bread, crumbed
2 eggs, beaten
2 tablespoons milk
1 cup grated cheese
Salt and pepper to taste

Method:

- Preheat the oven to 180°C.
- Mix the potatoes, spring onions, bread crumbs, eggs and milk.
- Season to taste and add half the grated cheese.
- Spoon the mixture into an ovenproof dish and bake for 20 minutes.
- Sprinkle the remaining cheese and bake for 5 minutes more.
- Serve hot.

A good recipe for days when your refrigerator seems rather empty of vegetables.

Potato Manchurian

Ingredients:

For the rolls:
4 medium potatoes, boiled and mashed
3-4 tablespoons cornflour
1 teaspoon chopped garlic
1 teaspoon chopped ginger
1 green chilly, chopped
Salt and pepper to taste
Oil for deep frying

For the sauce:
1 tablespoon chopped garlic
1 tablespoon chopped ginger
1 tablespoon chopped green chilly
2 tablespoons soy sauce
2 tablespoons vinegar
2 cups stock
2 tablespoons cornflour dissolved in water
Salt, pepper ajinomoto
Chopped spring onion leaves to garnish

Method:

- Mix the potato along with the cornflour, garlic, ginger, chilly, salt and pepper.
- Make into rolls and deep fry in hot oil.
- Keep aside.
- To make the sauce, remove all but 1 tablespoon oil from the karahi and add in the garlic, ginger and chilly.
- Stir fry and add the soy sauce, vinegar and stock.
- Season and thicken with the cornflour paste.
- Pour over the potato balls, garnish with spring onion leaves and serve hot.

Always mix cornflour in cold water. Add this paste in a steady stream into the boiling stock stirring continuously to avoid lumps.

International Main Course

Potatoes Siciliana

Ingredients:

3-4 potatoes, boiled and sliced
2 onions, sliced
2 capsicums, sliced
4 cloves garlic, crushed
4 tomatoes, peeled and chopped

Salt, pepper, chilly powder to taste
2 tablespoons oil
½ teaspoon mixed herbs
4 tablespoons grated cheese to garnish

Method:

- Heat the oil in a pan and stir fry the onions and capsicums.
- Drain and remove.
- In the same oil, stir fry the garlic and add in the chopped tomatoes.
- Cook well, mashing up the tomatoes.
- Season with salt, pepper, chilli powder and herbs.
- Add in the sliced potatoes along with the onions and capsicums and heat through.
- Sprinkle with cheese before serving.

Potato Pesto Bake

Ingredients:

8 potatoes, thickly sliced
1 cup fresh basil leaves
2 cloves garlic, crushed
2 tablespoons pinenuts/walnuts
4 tablespoons olive oil
4 tablespoons grated cheese
1 tablespoon flour
2 cups milk
Salt and pepper to taste
Grated cheese to garnish

Method:

- Boil the potato slices in salted water until almost done.
- Drain and layer onto an ovenproof dish.
- To make the pesto, place the basil, garlic, nuts, oil and cheese in a blender and process until smooth.
- Whisk the flour into the milk and cook over high heat stirring continuously until thick.
- Whisk in the blended pesto and pour over the potatoes.
- Sprinkle over the extra cheese and bake or grill for about 10 minutes until brown.
- Serve hot.

You can also serve this Pesto sauce over cooked pasta or a mixture of lightly steamed vegetables like broccoli, zucchini, red and yellow peppers and baby carrots.

ONE DISH MEALS

Potato Pizza

Ingredients:
4 potatoes, scrubbed
Salt and pepper
2-3 tablespoons oil
For the topping:
2-3 tablespoons tomato sauce

Mushroom slices, capsicum slices, black olives
3-4 tablespoons grated cheese

Method:
- Grate the potatoes coarsely.
- Season with salt and pepper.
- Warm a frying pan and add in a tablespoon of oil.
- When the oil is hot, put in all the grated potato and press it down to make a flat round cake.
- Cover the pan and cook till the base is golden brown.
- Turn the pancake around and fry the other side adding more oil as necessary.
- Place the pancake on a heatproof plate and spread the tomato sauce on top.
- Sprinkle the grated cheese and arrange the vegetables on top.
- Grill or bake for 10 minutes until the cheese has melted.
- Serve hot.

Potato and Mushroom Enchiladas

Ingredients:

2 potatoes, boiled
1 packet mushroom
1 onion, chopped
3-4 cloves garlic, crushed
1 capsicum, chopped
4 tomatoes
½ teaspoon chilly powder
½ teaspoon pepper
¼ teaspoon jeera powder
Salt to taste
2 tablespoons oil

1 cup grated cheese
8 tortillas
For the sauce:
1 onion, chopped
8 cloves garlic, chopped
6-8 tomatoes
2 teaspoons sugar
¼ teaspoon chilli powder
Salt and pepper to taste
2 tablespoons oil
Coriander leaves to garnish

Method:

- To prepare the sauce, heat the oil in a pan and stir fry the onion and garlic.
- Peel and chop the tomatoes and add to the pan.
- Add in the sugar, chilli, salt and pepper.
- Cover and cook for about 10-15 minutes.
- For the filling, peel and cut the potatoes into cubes and slice the mushrooms.
- Heat the oil in a frying pan and fry the potatoes until golden. Remove.
- Add the onion and the garlic to the same oil and stir fry.
- Add the mushrooms along with the capsicum and cook for a few minutes more.
- Peel and chop the tomatoes and add to the pan along with the potatoes.
- Season with the chilly, jeera, salt and pepper and stir well.
- Mix in half the grated cheese and divide the filling between the tortillas.
- Roll the tortillas and place in an ovenproof dish.
- Top with the sauce and the remaining grated cheese and bake in a preheated oven for 20 minutes until the cheese melts.
- Serve hot garnished with coriander leaves.

Baked Potato

Ingredients:

4 large potatoes, scrubbed
Coleslaw
Hung Curd
Baked Beans
Cooked Corn
Stir Fried Mushrooms

Grated cheese
Grated Paneer
Butter
Pepper
Salt

Method:

- Prick the potatoes, wrap each individually into foil parcels and bake at 180°C for 1-1/2 hours, until the potatoes are cooked.
- Split open the potatoes and serve with one or more of the above toppings.

Potato Gado Gado Salad

Ingredients:

2 potatoes, boiled
1 carrot
8-10 French beans
4-5 cauliflower florettes
½ cup shredded cabbage
1 cucumber, sliced
1 cup cooked rice
Lettuce leaves to garnish

For the dressing:
½ cup roasted peanuts
8 cloves garlic, chopped
1 onion, chopped
1 lemon juice
2 teaspoons sugar
1 teaspoon chilly powder
Salt to taste

Method:
- Peel and cut the potatoes into strips.
- Cut the beans and carrots diagonally and steam along with the cauliflower.
- Allow to cool while preparing the dressing.
- Grind the peanuts finely adding ½ cup of water.
- Warm the oil in a pan and lightly fry the onion and garlic.
- Add ½ cup water, chilly powder sugar, salt and peanut paste.
- Boil and simmer for a few minutes until the dressing is creamy.
- Remove from the fire and add in the lemon juice.
- Arrange the lettuce and vegetables on a platter.
- Surround the vegetables with the rice and the potatoes.
- Pour over the dressing and serve.

One Dish Meals

Spanish Omlette

Ingredients:

2 potatoes, peeled and thinly sliced
2 onions, chopped
1 capsicum, chopped
1 tomato, chopped
100 gms mushrooms, sliced
6 eggs
3-4 tablespoons oil
Salt and pepper to taste

Method:

- Heat 2 tablespoons oil and add in the onions, capsicum and potatoes.
- Add salt to taste, cover and cook.
- Add in the mushrooms and tomato and stir fry.
- Meanwhile, whisk the eggs and mix in the vegetables along with additional salt and pepper to taste.
- Rinse the pan and add 1 tablespoon of oil.
- Heat and pour in the egg mixture.
- Cover and cook on a low flame till the underside is brown.
- Flip the omlette over using more oil if necessary.
- Cook the other side.
- Remove, cut into wedges and serve hot.

Aloo Frankee Rolls

Ingredients:

4 potatoes, boiled
1 onion finely chopped
2 green chillies, finely chopped
2 tablespoons coriander leaves, chopped
½ lemon juice
½ teaspoon jeera powder
Salt to taste
1 cup flour
1 cup atta
4-6 tablespoons oil
Green chutney to serve

Method:

- Mash the potatoes and add the onion, green chilly, coriander leaves, lemon juice, jeera powder and salt to taste.

- Mix the flour and atta along with salt and rub in the oil.
- Knead to a soft dough using water.
- Roll out portions of the dough into thin chapaties.
- Cook on a hot tava till light specks appear on both sides.
- Keep warm.
- Take a chapati at a time and spread chutney on it.
- Spread a portion of the potato mixture and roll.
- Repeat the same with the remaining chapatis.

Potato Pancake Rolls

Ingredients:

1 cup atta
1 egg
1½ cups milk
1-2 tablespoons oil

For the filling:
1 onion, finely chopped
1 green chilly, chopped
2 potatoes, boiled
1 tablespoon flour
1 cup milk
1 tablespoon butter or oil
Salt and pepper to taste

Method:
- Prepare the filling by gently frying the onion and chilly in butter.
- Peel and dice the potatoes and add to the pan.
- Whisk the milk and flour and add in, stirring continuously until the sauce is thick.
- Season with salt and pepper and keep aside.
- Prepare the batter for the pancakes by whisking together the atta, egg and milk.
- Add salt to taste.
- Brush a non stick frying pan with a little oil.
- Pour a ladleful of batter and tilt the pan to coat the bottom evenly.
- Cook till brown, then turn over and cook the other side.
- Remove and repeat with the remaining batter.
- Divide the filling equally between the pancakes, roll up and serve.

Potato Pancake

Ingredients:

4 potatoes, scrubbed
1 large onion
6 tablespoons flour
4 eggs
Salt and pepper
Oil for shallow frying
For the topping:
1 cup thick dahi

1 tablespoon finely chopped onion
1 tablespoon finely chopped capsicum
1 finely chopped green chilly
Finely chopped coriander
Salt to taste

Method:
- Mix all the ingredients for the topping and set aside.
- Grate the potatoes coarsely.
- Grate the onion and mix with the potatoes, along with the salt and pepper.
- Add in the eggs and the flour and make a batter.
- Heat a little oil in a frying pan and fry tablespoons of the mixture until golden brown.
- Turn over and fry the other side adding more oil as necessary.
- Serve hot along with the topping.

Eggs Flamenco

Ingredients:

4 tablespoons oil
1 onion, chopped
1 capsicum, chopped
2 potatoes, boiled and diced
½ cup green peas

4 tomatoes, chopped
Chopped parsley/coriander
Salt and pepper to taste
4 eggs

Method:
- Heat the oil in a frying pan and add the onion and capsicum.
- Stir fry for 3-4 minutes and add in the potatoes, green peas, tomatoes and

One Dish Meals

parsley.
- Season with salt and pepper and cook, covered on a low flame.
- Turn the vegetable mixture into a shallow ovenproof dish.
- Make 4 hollows in the mixture and break an egg into each one.
- Cook in a preheated oven at 180°C for 15 minutes, until the egg whites are set.
- Serve immediately.

Potato Kathee Rolls

Ingredients:
Whole wheat flour
Milk
Salt to taste
1 teaspoon sugar
Pinch of elaichi powder
For the topping (optional):
Hung yogurt
Coriander leaves
For the filling:
4-5 boiled potatoes

1 teaspoon jeera
2 teaspoons grated ginger
1-2 green chillies chopped
2 capsicums chopped
3-4 chopped tomatoes
salt, pepper, garam masala
kasoori methi

Method:
- Knead the flour with the flavouring and the milk.
- Make balls and roll out into chappaties using ghee or oil if needed.
- For the filling, peel and cut the potatoes into cubes.
- Heat the oil in a pan and add the jeera, green chilly and ginger.
- Add the tomato, salt and pepper.
- Add chopped capsicum, kasoori methi, garam masala and potato cubes.
- Fill the mix into chappaties and make rolls.
- Serve hot with hung curd and garnished with coriander leaves.

CHAATS

Diet Aloo Chaat

Ingredients:

4 potatoes, boiled
½ cup fresh anaar seeds
1 lemon juice
2 teaspoons chaat masala

Salt to taste
Other fresh fruits eg. pineapple, apple, banana, orange etc.

Method:

- Peel and cut the potatoes into cubes.
- Mix in the anaar, lemon juice, chaat masala and salt to taste.
- Chill and serve.

To make a chatpata chaat masala, lightly roast 2 tbsp dhania seeds, 2 dry red chillies, 4 tbsp jeera seeds and 1 tbsp black pepper corns. Cool and grind along with 2 tbsp amchoor powder, 1 tbsp black salt and salt to taste.

Bread Aloo Bhel

Ingredients:

8 slices bread
½ cup sev
2 onions, chopped
2 potatoes, boiled
1 cup kurmura
Sweet chutney

Chilly chutney
Lassan chutney (optional)
Lemon juice
Coriander leaves and sev to garnish

Method:
- Cut the slices of bread into cubes and deep fry.
- Peel and cut the potatoes into cubes.
- Mix the bread, sev, onions and potatoes together with the kurmura.
- Mix in the chutneys to taste along with a squeeze of lemon juice.
- Serve immediately garnished with coriander leaves and extra sev.

If your kurmura is not too crisp, put it in a bowl into the microwave and heat on high for 2-3 minutes.

Aloo Paapdi Chaat

Ingredients:

20 -25 paapdis
2 potatoes, boiled
½ cup kabuli channa
1 cup moong sprouts
2 cups dahi
Sweet chutney

Chilly powder
Jeera powder
Salt to taste
Sev
Coriander leaves

Method:
- Soak the kabuli channa overnight.
- Cook with salt to taste.
- Peel and slice the potatoes.
- Lightly steam the moong sprouts.
- Spread the paapdis on a serving tray.
- Arrange the potatoes, channa and moong sprouts over the paapdis.
- Sprinkle the sweet chutney over.
- Whisk the dahi with salt and spread over the paapdis.
- Sprinkle the chilly and jeera powders.
- Garnish with sev and coriander leaves and serve immediately.

Biscuit Chaat

Ingredients:

1 packet salty biscuits
½ cup boondi
1 onion, chopped
1 tomato, chopped
2 potatoes, boiled

Sweet chutney
Chilly chutney
1 teaspoon chaat masala
Coriander leaves to garnish

Method:
- Peel and chop the potatoes.
- Bread the biscuits into small pieces.
- Toss the broken biscuits, boondi, onion, tomato and potato together.
- Mix in the sweet and chilly chutneys to taste.
- Sprinkle the chaat masala, garnish with coriander leaves and serve immediately.

A chatpata snack to serve kids when they get back from school. Lower in calories too as the fried papdis are missing.

Chaats

Berhampuri Papdi Chaat

Ingredients:

For the Ragda:
1 cup dried white peas
1 teaspoon grated ginger
2 tomatoes, chopped
½ teaspoon chilly powder
½ teaspoon dhania powder
½ teaspoon jeera powder
Salt to taste

For the Chaat:
15 -20 papdis
3-4 potatoes, boiled
1 cup dahi
1 onion, chopped
¼ teaspoon chilly powder
¼ teaspoon jeera powder
Salt to taste
Sweet chutney
Chilly chutney
Sev to garnish

Method:
- Soak the peas overnight.
- Add the remaining ingredients and cook until soft.
- Peel and slice the potatoes.
- To serve, divide the ragda between 4 plates.
- Top with potato slices.
- Whisk the dahi with salt and pour about 2 tablespoons each over the potato slices.
- Sprinkle over the onion, jeera and chilly powders.
- Add the sweet and chilly chutney to taste.
- Crush the papdis and garnish the chaat with the papdis and sev and serve immediately.

Banarasi Aloo Chaat

Ingredients:

4-5 potatoes, boiled
Sweet chutney
Chilly chutney
½ Chilly powder
½ Jeera powder

½ cup dahi
Crushed paapdis
Salt to taste
Oil for shallow frying

Method:

- Peel and cut the potatoes into large cubes.
- Heat 2 tablespoons oil in a flat pan and fry the potato cubes a few at a time.
- Toss the hot potatoes with the sweet and chilly chutneys along with chilly, jeera and salt to taste.
- Distribute the potatoes into serving plates, top with dahi and crushed paapdis and serve immediately.

To make papdis take a cup of flour and rub into it about 2 tbsp of oil. Add salt to taste and enough water to make a soft dough. Knead well and roll out into small thin rounds about 4 cms in diameter. Prick with a fork and deep fry in hot oil.

Sprout Bhel

Ingredients:

2 cups mixed sprouts
2 potatoes, boiled
1 onion, chopped
1 cucumber, chopped
1 tomato, chopped
1 carrot, grated
100 gms paneer, chopped

1 green chilly, chopped
1 teaspoon chaat masala
Salt to taste
Lemon juice
Coriander leaves
Fresh pudina

Method:
- Lightly steam or boil the sprouts until still crunchy.
- Cool.
- Peel and chop the potatoes and mix with the onion,
- Cucumber, tomato, carrot, paneer and green chilly.
- Mix the vegetables with the sprouts, adding chaat masala and salt to taste.
- Add the lemon juice and chopped coriander and mint leaves and serve.

To make sprouts, put the pulses into a bowl, cover with cold water and leave to soak overnight. Drain and tie loosely in a piece of cloth until they sprout.

Aloo Vada Chaat

Ingredients:

For the Vadas:
4 potatoes, boiled
½ teaspoon rye
Curry leaves
½ teaspoon ginger paste
½ teaspoon garlic paste
2 green chillies, chopped
½ teaspoon haldi powder
2 tablespoons coriander leaves
Salt to taste
1 cup besan
Oil for deep frying

For serving:
2 cups dahi
Sweet chutney
Chilly chutney
1 potato, boiled
Sev for garnishing
Crushed paapdis
Coriander leaves
Salt to taste

Method:

For the vadas:
- Peel and coarsely mash the potatoes.
- Heat a teaspoon of oil and splutter the rye and curry leaves.
- Stir fry the ginger, garlic, green chilly and haldi powder and add to the potatoes.
- Mix the potatoes along with the coriander leaves and salt to taste and make into medium size balls.
- Mix the besan with water and salt to taste to make a thick batter.
- Heat the oil in a karahi.
- Dip the potato balls into the batter and deep fry until golden.

To serve:
- Whisk the dahi along with salt to taste and pour into a flat dish.
- Slit the vadas into 4 and place on the dahi.
- Slice the extra potato and place the slices around the vadas.
- Sprinkle the sweet and chilly chutneys over the vadas.
- Garnish with sev, crushed paapdis and coriander leaves before serving.

Aloo Corn Bhel

Ingredients:

2 potatoes, boiled
2 cups sweet corn kernels, boiled
1 onion, chopped
1 capsicum, chopped
2 green chillies, chopped
½ teaspoon jeera powder
1 tablespoon oil
1 lemon
Salt to taste
Sev and coriander leaves to garnish

Method:

- Peel and cut the potatoes into cubes.
- Heat the oil in a pan and stir fry the onion, capsicum and green chilly for a few minutes.
- Add the potatoes, corn and jeera powder along with salt to taste and mix well.
- Remove from heat and squeeze in the lemon juice.
- Garnish with the sev and coriander leaves before serving.

Aloo Palak Chaat

Ingredients:

For the bhajias:
2 potatoes, thinly sliced
8-10 spinach leaves
½ cup besan
½ teaspoon chilly powder
Salt to taste
Oil for deep frying

For serving:
1 cup dahi
Salty boondi
Sweet chutney
Chilly chutney
Jeera powder

Method:
- Heat the oil in a karahi.
- Mix the besan along with salt, chilly powder and water to make a thin batter.
- Dip the potato slices and spinach leaves in the batter and deep fry until crisp.
- To serve, crush the bhajias and place on individual serving plates.
- Top with a spoon of dahi along with sweet and chilly chutney to taste.
- Garnish with the boondi and jeera powder and serve immediately.

To make jeera powder, roast jeera seeds in a karahi over a low flame, stirring occasionally until brown. Cool and grind coarsely.

Ragda Patties

Ingredients:

For the Ragda:
1 cup dried white peas
1 teaspoon grated ginger
2 green chillies
½ teaspoon dhania powder
½ teaspoon jeera powder
½ teaspoon haldi powder
Salt to taste

For the patties:
4 potatoes, boiled
3-4 slices bread, crumbed
1 green chilly, finely chopped
¼ teaspoon garam masala powder
¼ teaspoon haldi powder
Salt to taste
Oil for shallow frying

For serving:
Sweet chutney,
Chilly chutney,
chopped onions,
coriander leaves,
crushed papris

Method:

For the Ragda:
- Soak the peas overnight.
- Pressure cook the peas with about 3-4 cups of water along with the remaining ingredients until soft.

For the patties:
- Peel and mash the potatoes.
- Mix in the bread, green chilly, garam masala, haldi and salt and knead well.
- Heat about a tablespoon of oil in a frying pan.
- Make small patties with the potato mixture and shallow fry, using more oil as necessary.

To serve:
- Place 4-6 tablespoons of the hot ragda onto a flat plate.
- Place 2 of the patties on the ragda and sprinkle the sweet and chilly chutneys to taste.
- Garnish with chopped onions, coriander leaves and crushed papris and serve immediately.

Green Chilly Chutney

Ingredients:

15 - 18 green chillies
½ cup coriander
1 tablespoon sev
Salt to taste

Method:
- Grind all the ingredients to a paste in a blender.
- Store in an airtight bottle. When needed, thin the chutney down using a little water.

Sweet Tamarind Chutney

Ingredients:

100 gms imly
500 gms gur (jaggery)
2 cups water
½ teaspoon red chilli powder
2 teaspoons jeera powder
1 teaspoon black salt
1 teaspoon salt
½ teaspoon garam masala powder

Method:
- Soak the imly in hot water for 30 minutes. Blend the pulp in a mixie and strain.
- Add the remaining ingredients and bring to a boil. Cool and store.

Red Lassan Chutney

Ingredients:

8-10 cloves garlic
4 dry red chillies
½ teaspoon jeera
Salt to taste

Method:
- Grind all the ingredients to a paste using a little water.

FASTING

Aloo Khichidi

Ingredients:

4-5 potatoes, peeled
½ cup peanuts
2-3 green chillies
1 teaspoon ginger, chopped
1 teaspoon jeera
1 teaspoon sugar
Salt to taste
2 tablespoons oil
Coriander leaves
Grated coconut to garnish

Method:

- Grate the potatoes thickly and soak in cold water.
- Coarsely grind the peanuts and green chillies.
- Heat the oil in a karahi and splutter the jeera.
- Add in the ginger and peanut mixture and stir fry for a minute.
- Drain and add in the grated potatoes.
- Add the sugar along with salt to taste and mix well.
- Cover the karahi and allow to cook stirring frequently until the potatoes are cooked.
- Serve hot, garnished with coriander leaves and grated coconut.

Sabudana Vada

Ingredients:

2 potatoes, boiled
1 cup sabudana
½ cup roasted peanuts
2-3 green chillies
1 teaspoon jeera

1 teaspoon sugar
1 lemon juice
Salt to taste
Oil for deep frying

Method:

- Place the sabudana in a colander and soak by washing in running water.
- Drain and leave covered for 4-5 hours.
- Crush the peanuts, chillies and jeera coarsely.
- Peel and mash the potatoes in a bowl.
- Mix in the peanuts, adding sugar, lemon juice and salt to taste.
- Mix in the soaked sabudana.
- Heat the oil in a karahi until almost smoking.
- Form small balls of the vada mixture and flatten them.
- Deep fry until golden brown.
- Drain and serve hot with green chutney.

Grind together 1 cup coriander leaves, 3-4 green chillies, ½ tsp sugar, ½ tsp jeera, 1 tbsp roasted peanuts, ½ lemon juice and salt to taste to make green chutney.

Sabudana Khichdi

Ingredients:

2 cups sabudana
2 potatoes
1 teaspoon jeera
½ cup roasted peanuts
2 green chillies
½ teaspoon sugar
1 lemon juice
Salt to taste
3-4 tablespoons oil
Grated coconut to garnish

Method:

- Place the sabudana in a colander and soak by washing in running water.
- Drain and leave covered for about 4-5 hours.
- Peel and cut the potatoes into small cubes.
- Crush the peanuts and green chillies coarsely.
- Heat the oil in a karahi and add in the jeera.
- Add in the potato cubes and cook until done.
- Add in the peanuts and stir fry for a minute.
- Meanwhile mix the sugar, lemon juice and salt into the sabudana.
- Add the sabudana mixture into the karahi and mix well.
- Allow to cook, stirring occasionally until the sabudana turns translucent.
- Garnish with coconut and serve hot.

Stuffed Aloo Tikki

Ingredients:

4-5 potatoes, boiled
4-5 tablespoons grated coconut
4-5 tablespoons chopped coriander leaves
1 teaspoon ginger, finely chopped
2 green chillies, chopped
½ teaspoon jeera powder
Salt to taste
Oil for shallow frying

Method:

- Peel and mash the potatoes adding salt to taste.
- In another bowl, mix together the coconut, coriander leaves, ginger, green chilly, jeera powder and salt to taste.

Fasting

- Using a little oil, grease your hands and take a lemon sized portion of the mashed potato.
- Flatten and place a teaspoon of the coconut filling in it.
- Bring the potato together and make into a small ball.
- Flatten and leave aside.
- Repeat with the remaining potato and filling.
- Heat a non stick frying pan or tava and spread a teaspoon of oil.
- Place these stuffed tikkis on the tava and shallow fry using a little oil.
- Gently turn over and fry the other side in the same way.
- Serve hot with green chutney.

Sabudana Paratha

Ingredients:

1 cup sabudana, finely ground
½ cup sabudana
2 potatoes, boiled
½ cup peanuts
4-5 green chillies
1 teaspoon sugar
Salt to taste
Oil for shallow frying

Method:
- Place the ½ cup sabudana in a colander and soak by washing under running water.
- Drain and leave covered for 4-5 hours.
- Soak the sabudana powder in ½ cup water for 15-20 minutes.
- Coarsely grind the peanuts and green chillies.
- Peel and mash the potatoes.
- Mix the sabudana paste, soaked sabudana, potatoes, green chilly and peanuts and knead the mixture to a soft dough adding the sugar and salt to taste.
- Rub a little oil on your hands and take a lemon sized ball of the dough and flatten to form a thick paratha.
- Place this paratha on a heated tava and shallow fry using a teaspoon of oil.
- Turn over and cook the other side until both sides are golden brown.
- Repeat with the remaining dough and serve hot.

Acknowledgements

My heartfelt thanks to all those people who have made this "Work of Love" possible.

First of all, my family who has always had more faith in my abilities than I have in myself.

My thanks to my friend Dr. Suniti Deshpande who introduced me to my publisher.

My thanks to Indira Khanna for all her valuable suggestions and ideas.

And last but not the least my thanks to my photographer Prabhat Gupta for his most valuable support and efforts in making **"Mr. Potato"** the **Hero**.